Steps to the Sea

Ear Training and Composing in a Minute Equal Temperament

Julia Werntz

All audio examples, as well as the "Interval Survey Chart" PDF cited on page 11, and the PDF with notated illustrations of all of the "Listening Examples /Practice Exercises" cited on page 14, can be downloaded in a zip file at the following URL:
http://tinyurl.com/stepstothesea

My sincere thanks to Mat Maneri for his excellent work recording the audio examples for Part 2, to Andrea Gaudette for her reading and comments, and to Pandelis Karayorgis for his reading and comments as well as his audio editing.

Introduction

The following pages are intended to provide a way into organized microtonal hearing, thinking, and composing. All of the exercises and analysis are derived from more than two decades I have spent composing, studying, and teaching with microtones—the latter at the New England Conservatory in Boston. The ideas proposed here come from prolonged, extensive observation of professional and student musicians' experience working with tiny microintervals.

These days there is a great deal of theory regarding microtones, primarily based on acoustics, but I am deliberately sidestepping much of this, giving precedence instead to the practicing musician's point of view. By doing so I am asserting my faith in the skills of the well-trained musician and my belief that our own subjective listening experiences and careful observations will be of the greatest value. The ideas in this manual are only "theory" in the same sense that the study of counterpoint or part writing is theory, in that they point toward some guiding principles for *composition* with microtones. Furthermore, while those older disciplines are based on centuries of common practice, my exercises have been developed from within a comparatively small period; even now, more than a century after the first explorations, microtonal composition is still a very young and developing field, and there is no common practice. For this reason the best I can do is to point out my observations and encourage students to listen carefully, be thoughtful, and form their own systems of musical logic and aesthetics, their own microtonal styles.

Part 1 contains exercises for hearing and classifying the new intervals and Part 2 contains rudimentary compositional exercises designed to further develop and reinforce the student's understanding and hearing. But first some words about the context.

Why Are We Doing This?

Musicians are drawn to microtones for a variety of reasons—sometimes with rationales or philosophies that might even seem contradictory. For example, some relish the idea of music that sounds "out of tune," while others desire to make their music more "purely tuned." I believe that what I present in this manual can be useful no matter what one's reasons are. However, for the sake of clarity it is important for me to mention three premises that underlie my approach.

The first premise is that *pleasure or fascination with the sound is the essential motivating force* behind our choice to use microtones; that our senses, rather than arguments or concepts, will provide the most fruitful artistic path. Microintervals offer a rich resource for new types of melodies and harmonies, and thus they allow strange new modes of musical human expression to come forth.[1] Even for those who come to microtones through an intellectual rather than sensory route, one hopes that underneath it all the ear of the composer is stimulated, and that, ultimately, the ear of the listener will be, too. Arnold Schoenberg, musing on the microtonal music of the future in his 1922 *Harmonielehre*, showed great foresight on this matter when he speculated: "It will not come through reasoning, but from elemental sources; it will not come from without, but from within." [2,3]

The second premise is such an obvious corollary to the first one that it might not seem necessary to mention it: it is that *what we do with our new pitches is meant to be heard and felt,* that on some level the listener is meant to be aware of these new identities. We can assume this to be the case whether one is attempting a strongly unfamiliar or expressive sound or simply trying to imbue the music with pure intervals or certain mathematical ratios. Yet the audibility of microintervals is not guaranteed; whether or not we hear and feel them depends upon various factors in how we compose and perform them. When we use microtones we are going to a lot of effort—and asking our performers to go to a lot of effort—in order to do something different from what is standard practice. If the listener's experience in the end is essentially no different from what it would have been if the standard twelve equal-tempered pitches had been used, then all of this work has gone to waste, and the "microtonal effort" has failed. Therefore, while it may seem like a crude or pedestrian question—can we hear it or not?—it nonetheless demands our constant attention.

The third premise, in turn, arises naturally from the second; it is that *for any composer who really wants to compose microtonally, careful ear training should be the starting point.* As artists we must have an intimate working knowledge of our materials; if *we* cannot really hear our own intervals, how can we assume that anyone else will? Indeed, we might look skeptically at any composer working in standard twelve-note equal temperament who lacked the traditional basic ear training, yet such training has often been passed over by composers using microtones. Sometimes the aim with microtones is to make the sense of pitch itself blurry (accomplished easily with clusters or glissandi), or to use a loose, indefinite type of "quarter-tone" as a kind of effect in music that is otherwise using standard tuning (embellishing pitches that serve their purpose as long as they are somewhere in the middle regions between the twelve equal tempered pitches), and in such cases probably this sort of diligence isn't necessary. But when the desire is for intervals more specific and more integral to the music, then ear training will provide a solid stepping-stone into informed, realistic microtonal compositional practice, keeping the composer closely tied to the recipients of the music—the listeners and performers.

72 Equal Temperament

The microtonal scheme we will be using is 72 Equal Temperament (from now on referred to as 72 ET), so our smallest interval is one twelfth-tone, or about 17 cents (16.66 cents). Although we will stick to this temperament, the basic principles for ear training and thinking will be generally applicable to other fine microtonal octave divisions, even if they differ a bit in interval size.[4]

Some background
72 ET, as an idea, has a history that dates back to antiquity. The twelfth tone exists *in theory* in the tetrachords of Greek music theorist Aristoxenus of the 4th century BCE. As some of his scale steps involved quarter-tones, three quarter-tones, etc. and others involved sixth- and third-tones, the twelfth-tone was implied as the difference between these, the common denominator, even if it was not conceived of as a melodic interval in its own right.[5] Similarly, in the scales of Byzantine liturgical music the twelfth-tone is a theoretical unit, the *morion*, from which larger scale steps of differing sizes are derived—e.g. "tones" of 10, 12 or 14 *moria* and "semitones" of 4, 6 or 8.

In the history of modern microtonal music, 72 ET has been embraced by only a few. Russian microtonal pioneer Ivan Wyschnegradsky (1893-1979) dreamed about dividing the octave into seventy-two intervals, though he was not optimistic about the feasibility of performance—an understandable concern considering how infrequently even his quartertonal music was performed while he was alive. He did compose a piece in 72 ET for six pianos tuned a twelfth-tone apart, his *Arc-en-ciel*, in 1956 (with a second version in 1972)—though this didn't finally have its premiere performance until 1988, nine years after his death, in Graz. Meanwhile in the United States, since the 1960s and 1970s 72 ET has been used extensively in Boston by both Ezra Sims and Joseph Maneri (1927-2009), and a number of Maneri's former students, including myself. Though I'll discuss both Sims and Maneri more later, it's worth noting here that because of their years of work coaching, teaching, and collaborating with musicians in Boston (as well as New York and sporadically elsewhere), both composers and the performers they've worked with have been responsible for introducing the *viability of instrumental performance in 72 ET*, and thus raising the bar on microtonal performance in a broader sense. The Boston Microtonal Society has been actively cultivating this and other kinds of microtonal performance in its concerts and workshops since it was formed by Maneri and his students in 1989, and in 2006 the BMS formed its own microtonal chamber ensemble, NotaRiotous. (Other groups in the Boston area who have on occasion performed Sims's 72 ET music include Boston Musica Viva, the Pro Arte Orchestra, the Boston Modern Orchestra Project, the Dinosaur Annex Ensemble, and Collage New Music.) Finally, the International Ekmelic Music Society in Salzburg was formed in 1981 by composers Franz Richter Herf and Rolf Maedel, who promoted the use of 72 ET. Their concern, like Sims's, was approximating the pure intervals of the harmonic series, although much smaller subsets of the chromatic were used to this end. Today the Society isn't as specifically oriented toward this tuning system, but it continues to be active with concerts and lectures on microtonal music, and a few of their affiliate composers still use pitches derived from 72, to simulate pure intervals.

What 72 ET looks like

Seventy-two equal divisions of the octave may seem like an overwhelming number, yet it can immediately seem more accessible when we think of it as a matter of dividing the semitone into six equal microintervals. A graphic illustration of these pitch space divisions, like the one shown on the bottom of Figure 1, can sometimes be helpful for musicians in the beginning as a visual aide. The lines of text on the left represent the seven pitches in-between and including B and C, and the chart in the middle, continuing the same lines, indicates the microintervals formed by these pitches. In addition to the terms "twelfth-tone," "sixth-tone," etc., Alexander Ellis's "cents" numbers are used for interval size, with the semitone of 100 as a reference. The twelfth-tone is 16.66 cents (17 cents), the sixth-tone is 33.33 cents (33 cents), and the quarter-tone is 50 cents. The text to the right illustrates how, if we continued upward from B or downward from C to the next larger intervals, we would have the third-tone of 66.66 (67) cents and the five-twelfths-tone of 83.33 (83) cents.

Figure 1. Cents numbers of 12 ET intervals; graphic illustration of semitone pitch space equally divided into twelfth-, sixth- and quarter-tones

m2	= 100 cents	P5	= 700 cents
M2	= 200 cents	m6	= 800 cents
m3	= 300 cents	M6	= 900 cents
M3	= 400 cents	m7	= 1000 cents
P4	= 500 cents	M7	= 1100 cents
A4/d5	= 600 cents	P8	= 1200 cents

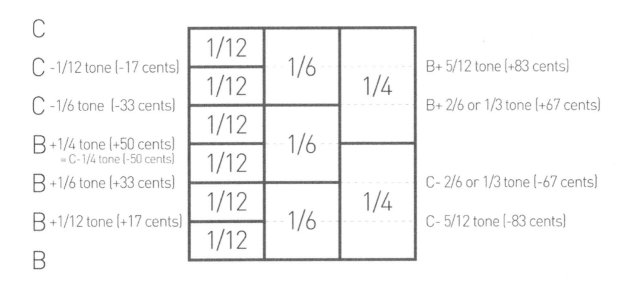

From the performer's angle it is even simpler, especially with a comprehensible notational system such as the one we'll be using, designed by Ezra Sims in the 1960s and shown in Figure 2. Note that in this system, since there is no symbol for raising or lowering a pitch by anything larger than a quarter-tone, the quarter-tone is thus the only microinterval that has two enharmonic equivalents in the notation; the rest have only one symbol. This limits the work for the performer in an important way, since there are just three degrees of raising a pitch and three degrees of lowering a pitch. (After raising B, in our example, by one twelfth-tone, one sixth-tone and one quarter-tone, rather than continuing to think and bend the pitch further upwards to one third-tone and five twelfths, instead the performer is *lowering C* by those same degrees of sixth-tone or twelfth-tone.) This orientation takes most kinds of instrumental technique and training into account. There are some exceptions, such as brass instruments with which lowering pitches is often easier to achieve than raising them, or standard fretted string instruments with which bending pitches is most easily done *upward* by increasing tension (pulling the string across the neck), while decreasing tension to lower the pitch presents a challenge. Nonetheless students report that as they negotiate these technical hurdles they are grateful for a notation system that builds upon their training oriented around the notes on the staff and the upward/downward accidentals and interval divisions.

Figure 2. Ezra Sims's microtonal symbols; pitch rising by twelfth-tones from B to C; symbol combined with traditional accidental.

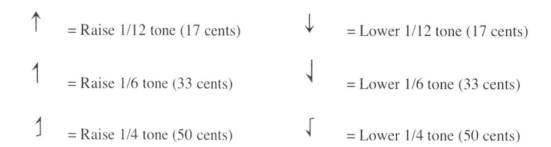

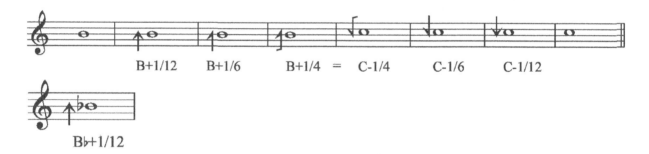

Though eventually composers (as well as singers without absolute pitch) need to learn to hear and think beyond this angle—hearing many new intervals rather than just three types of pitch inflections—thinking about it this way nonetheless can be helpful in the beginning, in understanding the structure of the temperament.

What 72 ET offers the musician

72 Equal Temperament creates a very fine grid. Here is what it offers the musician:

• Despite what newcomers often fear, *our smallest unit, one twelfth of a tone, can be distinguished clearly by the listener, and can be a potent melodic element previously unheard of.*

Audio Example 1: Violist Mat Maneri improvising with twelfth-tones.

On the other hand, the twelfth-tone is a fragile interval that, if treated carelessly, can be rendered imperceptible and pointless. Its power depends completely on how it is used, as we'll see later.

• Also contrary to common concerns, *the twelfth-tone is quite attainable on most instruments, including the voice* (and of course the same is true for the larger sixth- and quarter-tones). While we cannot know if a performer is playing *precisely* 16.66 cents, 33.33 cents, 50 cents, etc., most skilled performers can get within a few cents of these intervals, and that is our goal. (Readers may be relieved to learn this.) With practice, performers are quick to develop a reliable sense of what the twelfthtonal intervals sound and feel like to produce with the hands, lips, and voice, as distinct from the semitonal, the sixthtonal and the quartertonal, and this is especially the case if one has the opportunity to work with peers in a group. This kind of communal, shared knowledge of the intervals is formed annually among the students in my course at the New England Conservatory, and among any groups of performers who work together on the music (for example the players of the NotaRiotous ensemble).

• Within this grid we have a rich resource of *new interval combinations* and therefore *great flexibility*. With the combination of three twelfth-tones, quarter-tones are possible, and two twelfth-tones combined give us a sixth-tone. So then, contained within 72 ET we have the subsets of 24 ET (all quarter-tones), 36 ET (all sixth-tones), or even 18 ET (all third tones—a temperament that contains no semitones, minor thirds, perfect fourths or fifths, or major sixths or sevenths). A composer thus has the option of moving freely around with any combination of quarter-, sixth- and twelfthtonal intervals (as well as the traditional semitonal ones), or may at any moment choose instead to simplify things by using one of the subsets. And as is the case with any equal temperament, transposition of musical material is always possible—now in numerous new ways.

• With so many combinations we have *immensely expanded expressive possibilities*, which as has been stated earlier is presumed to be a primary reason for using microtones.

• Finally, it's important to note that with such a fine grid *it's possible to approximate most other tunings very closely*, since our pitches can never be more than 8.33 cents (one twenty-fourth of a tone) away from the pitches of any other system. For example, as was mentioned earlier, for those interested in pure intervals derived from the harmonic series—composers working in some form of either Spectralism or just intonation—72 ET would be valuable because it gets within 3 or 4 cents of the first eleven partials. The interval formed by the fifth partial and the fundamental is a major third of 386 cents, and 72 ET produces one of 383 cents, just 3 cents smaller; the seventh partial creates a minor seventh of 969 cents and our 967-cent seventh is only 2 cents smaller than that (just as our 700-cent fifth is 2 cents smaller than the pure fifth formed by the third partial); the eleventh partial creates a fourth of 551 cents, and our 550-cent fourth is only 1 cent smaller. The thirteenth partial diverges a bit more; at 840 cents it is 7 cents larger than our 833 cents, yet in the majority of contexts this is likely to be close enough for most ears. Whether one is interested in these types of intervals or intervals derived from various non-Western tunings, or some other source, a minute temperament such as this brings us so close that only the most rare listener would be able to tell the difference. Ezra Sims espouses this view. He recently wrote the following to me in an email: "Some people may have Korg-like [digital tuner] perception, but I don't and apparently few do... When I would exchange the computer JI [just intonation] realization of one of my own pieces for the 72-note ET version, it didn't bother me, no colleague remarked on it, and I would have defied anyone to tell a difference." Add to this the certainty that even the most precise performers will waver within a few cents of any target pitch, in any tuning, and 72 pitches to the octave can truly seem plentiful and very broadly applicable. To summarize: 72 ET can be a valuable choice because it is audible, it is attainable in performance, it substantially enhances the creative materials for the inspiration of the composer, and it is flexible and versatile—criteria that probably should be behind any choice of temperament. But in the end a temperament alone guarantees you nothing—perhaps it isn't even more interesting than cans of colored paints sitting on the shelf. Whether or not it *really* has value depends on the writing, and that's where the excitement lies.

Joseph Maneri and *Preliminary Studies in the Virtual Pitch Continuum*

This manual is in an outgrowth not only of my own teaching and composing, but also of my earlier years (late 1990s to early 2000s) co-teaching with my former teacher and close friend Joseph Maneri, and of his own method book *Preliminary Studies in the Virtual Pitch Continuum,* co-authored with Scott Van Duyne.[6] *Preliminary Studies*, published in 1986, was written by Maneri and Van Duyne during the first years of Maneri's course in Microtonal Composition and Performance at the New England Conservatory. Over the years the activities in Maneri's class evolved in such a way that some of the basic exercises in the book were favored while others were unused. Eventually, in the early 2000s, Maneri asked me to work on a new edition with him, and we began sketching some ideas, but the business of life prevented us from getting very far. In 2007, when Maneri retired and passed the course on to me, I began creating my own exercises for the students—some partially influenced by the *Preliminary Studies* exercises and some completely new. I view this manual in a sense as a delayed realization of that effort at a new edition of *Preliminary Studies*, even though the exercises, analysis and text are entirely my own rather than a collaboration with Joe. I have preserved certain important ideals from *Preliminary Studies*, beyond the use of 72 ET, and I'll list them here.

• The study being a practical one of microtonal composition, not of tuning.
• The absence of tonality as context, and the absence of traditional rhythmic/metric structures as well. Maneri knew that when suffusing our sound world with sixty new pitches, it is a mistake to presume that the structural logic of the music of the past can be superimposed onto it. However, whereas *Preliminary Studies* strictly forbade the existence of pitch centers of any kind, or even repeated pitches, that is not the case here.
• The idea that rudimentary compositional exercises and ear training occur and develop simultaneously, influencing each other.
• The assumption that melodic line, and the perception of distinct pitch relationships, are priorities. (There is much microtonal music in which this is not the case.)
• The idea of creating microtonal pitch sets—e.g. tetrachords or hexachords—and using them as a basis for various exercises. (However my hexachordal exercises are different from those in *Preliminary Studies*, and they are designed to further develop the sense of a recognizable identity for the pitch set.)

How to Use This Manual

Our points of departure are the twelve intervals of the Western scale, since they are today's musical "lingua franca." Therefore a solid background in standard Western intervallic ear training is a necessary prerequisite for this study. Training in Western harmony and counterpoint is *not* necessary. (Though with some experience in it, students might grasp certain concepts in this manual a bit more quickly.)

Part 1 provides ear training drills and a structure with which to begin classifying and organizing the microintervals. The exercises are grouped by microinterval type: quartertonal intervals first, then only sixthtonal intervals, then finally twelfthtonal. The same groupings are followed in the composition exercises in Part 2. It is recommended that the student stick to this path, taking the following approach: work with the quartertonal ear training exercises in Part 1, then proceed to the quartertonal composition exercises in Part 2; come back to Part 1 and follow the same process with sixthtonal intervals; repeat process a final time with the twelfthtonal intervals—mostly used in combination with sixth- and quarter-tones for real 72 ET composing. It should be noted that with music composed in 72 ET, the listener is unlikely to *hear* according to those preliminary categories (quartertonal intervals over here, sixthtonal over there, etc.), but will interpret the music according to how it is organized by the composer, and of course by how it measures against what he/she already knows of music. Nonetheless the stepwise approach in this section allows us a manageable, graduated entry, one element at a time, into the world of new pitch relationships.

The title "Steps to the Sea" ("Gradus ad Mare" in Latin) is a play on "Gradus ad Parnassum," which centuries ago was a common title for books offering step-by-step instruction in the fine arts, and was famously used by the Baroque composer Johann Joseph Fux for his counterpoint manual. It was invoked by Maneri and Van Duyne in their introduction to *Preliminary Studies in the Virtual Pitch Continuum*, as well. But while that title implies an ascent to the mountain of the Muses, the image that seems appropriate to my mind is that of motion outward, as one moves into the sea. Ezra Sims made the same sort of nautical analogy once, when describing Maneri's music and teaching, stating that he "sports freely in the whole sea of seventy-two-note possibilities."[7] Looking at it this way, we can ponder what we might find in this sea, remembering the strange creatures that are found out in the deeper waters, things not seen closer to the crowded shore. Stepping-stones have been carefully provided here to lead you out and back, and—I hope—a good swimming mask to help you see as you explore.

Part 1: Hearing and Classifying the Intervals

Preliminary Advice

Before beginning the exercises in Part 1, please note the following points of advice:

• **Reviewing 12 ET:** It is recommended that you make a quick review of the precise tuning of the twelve equal-tempered intervals before you begin the microintervals. Most well-trained musicians have spent years developing a reliable sense of the traditional intervals and their tuning, yet even when we have mastered this it is customary to inflect pitches a bit for expressive or coloristic effect, sometimes as much as a twelfth-tone or more. Therefore it is wise to review the sound of accurately tuned intervals in 12 ET. We may find, for example, that the semitone is not what we expected. Musicians often make the semitone somewhat smaller in melodic situations where it is a tendency-tone motion, such as the leading tone ascending to the tonic. This is so common, in fact, that musicians are often surprised when they hear an equal-tempered semitone of 100 cents; it feels larger than expected.[8]

• **Use of voice and instrument:** The ear training drills should be practiced both with the voice and on the instrument. The use of the voice is particularly important for composers, to ensure that we are really learning the full gamut of intervals within the octave, not merely the three types of pitch adjustment mentioned in the introduction.

• **Working with peers:** The ideal setting for all exercises in both Part 1 and Part 2 is to work with a partner or a small group of musicians if possible, so that you may check each other for consistency and accuracy. The input of your peers will help you develop your ear with greater confidence. It also will enable you to play and hear multiple lines simultaneously, as well as harmonies.

• **Making your own personal interval survey chart:** It is recommended that while proceeding through the exercises in Part 1 you keep a record of your impressions of the intervals in a personal survey chart of the sort provided on the PDF download shown at the front of book. Recording our initial impressions of the new sounds is of great value as we try to develop a sense of how *others* will perceive them. For example, descriptions like "twisted," "more vibrant," "crying," "sweeter, " or "darker" often come up, or resemblances to certain bird calls, doorbells, sirens, etc. Synesthetic musicians report visual associations, and one student claimed he *felt* a certain interval in his sinuses. (Iannis Xenakis stated in an interview that one of the reasons he used quarter-tones in his music was because

11

they "might produce a sound more alive."[9]) Though these descriptions may seem quite subjective, applying adjectives in this way is a good practice because it forces us to pay attention and attempt to characterize our reactions to the intervals. Furthermore, students often find that assigning descriptive terms can help them recall the intervals more reliably later. Again, working on this with a group and sharing impressions—as well as some solitary listening—is ideal.

Here are some issues you may have in mind as you explore your reactions to each interval and fill out the chart:

- **Can you hear it or not?** Sometimes the question is quite simple and elemental: can you even distinguish this interval as something other than one of the twelve equal-tempered ones?

- **Consonance and dissonance.** Consider the question of consonance and dissonance. Is it relevant to your music and thought? Will you be listening to the new intervals in terms of the sense of stability and instability they give? If so, it is best to take an honest approach to this survey. Is it really safe to assume—as many do—just because we know about the harmonic series, that we will always *hear* 383 cents (close to the 5/4) as a more "correct" major third than 400 cents or 367 cents, or 967 cents (close to the 7/4) as a more correct minor seventh than 983 cents or 950 cents, and so on? A blind study with the help of your peers would be the most informative for you on this matter. In one blind survey I did with students, several students in the class chose the sixth-tone large perfect fifth as preferable to the 700-cent one (pure, by 2 cents). What does "preferable" mean, and why did the students perceive it this way? There could be any number of explanations, but the important point is that the students' reaction shows again that the ear and the gut are the best guides for musical choice, rather than preconceived theories.

- **Beyond consonance and dissonance.** It is possible that you will find that the old two-pronged approach to classifying intervals—consonant or dissonant—is insufficient when trying to understand so many new intervals. Although clearly stable and clearly unstable sonorities don't cease to exist (e.g. perfect fifths, and beating intervals around the minor second and smaller), often the degree to which we experience them *on these terms* does not change dramatically with minute adjustments of a twelfth- or sixth-tone, especially in the context of most music—i.e. when they're not sustained for a long time in a two-voice texture. Furthermore, there will be intervals that simply don't seem to fit clearly into one category at the exclusion of the other. The importance of these two classifications therefore may fade.[10]

If so, your own characterizations, of the personal sort described above, will probably be more interesting and more useful, more directly relevant to your creative process as you begin to compose. There is plenty of historical precedent for the value of a subjective, descriptive approach to pitch materials, such as the "ethos" the ancient Greeks attributed to each of their scales, the specific emotions or properties musicians associate with different Arabic or Persian Maqams ("tragic," "spiritual," "masculine," "feminine," etc.), or the "key characteristics" popular in 18th- and 19th-Century Europe. Even today's much more simplistic terms for the standard intervals, such as "melancholy" or "sad" for minor third and minor sixth ("happy" for major), remind us of the important role that our emotions and imagination play in this process.

- **Factors affecting your perception.** Look for any trends in your reactions and thoughts. If you find any, what are they based on? Microinterval type? (Hearing all quartertonal intervals a certain way, all sixthtonal another way, etc.) Harmonic vs. melodic intervals? Ascending vs. descending forms? Microtonally augmenting vs. microtonally diminishing the traditional twelve intervals? Any of these factors may apply in certain cases and not in others.

Understanding how we hear pitch relationships is a complex process, made even more so by the introduction of microintervals. It is best attempted with small steps, recording your observations in this methodical way. In the end your chart may be incomplete, indecisive, messy and somewhat repetitive, but it will nonetheless be the most authentic and reliable resource for you as an artist.

• **"Harmonic Understanding" section:** The section titled "Harmonic Understanding," at the end of Part 1, is a discussion of the intervals and how they might be categorized. It is based not only on my own experience, but also on that of other musicians experienced in microtones, and it is meant to be thought-provoking rather than conclusive. Perhaps it is best to read it only after finishing your own personal interval chart, in order first to discover your own reactions to the new sounds.

Listening Examples /Practice Exercises

The audio examples here are grouped according to microtone type. For each microtone type there are two audio tracks—one demonstrating all of the intervals in the ascending melodic form (plus the harmonic form) and the other demonstrating all of the same intervals the descending melodic form (again plus the harmonic form). Each interval is presented five times in different arbitrary transpositions, as an exercise for practice. As you listen to the exercise for each interval you will hear the following four things in sequence (also illustrated in Figure 3):

1. The interval played melodically with no pause, for listening. (The first note is always a pitch from the 12 ET scale.)
2. The melodic interval repeated with a pause between the first note and the second. The pause is there to give you a chance to find the second pitch on your own with your voice or instrument, imitating what you've just heard. It is best if you repeat the starting pitch and then find the second pitch; this way you're producing the interval, not just a single pitch.
3. The same starting pitch of the interval alone and sustained, so that you can find and sustain the second pitch, and create the harmonic interval yourself.
4. The same two pitches sustained as a harmony, for listening.

Although the intervals within each microtone type are given in order from smallest to largest (e.g. 50 cents, then 150 cents, then 250 cents, etc.), you may choose to listen to them, practice them, and fill out your chart in any order—the order in which you're most curious to learn them.

Figure 3. Illustration of listening examples/practice exercises, using 233 cents ascending as an example. Normal noteheads indicate notes to be listened to, and smaller noteheads (stems down) indicate notes to be sung or played.

A second PDF, with all of the examples notated, is available for downloading at the URL shown at the front of the book.

After doing an exercise in all five transpositions (possibly repeating the exercise with the entire track a number of times), and describing your experience of the interval on your chart, a sense of the interval identity should begin to take hold. At this point you can begin to try the intervals on your own in new transpositions— with peers, ideally.

Quartertonal intervals

    Audio Example 2: ascending intervals of 50 to 1250 cents

    Audio Example 3: descending intervals of 50 to 1250 cents

    A few observations on quartertonal intervals: Of all the types of micro-intervals, quartertonal intervals sound the least like the semitonal intervals that neighbor them, and thus they have the most unique and unfamiliar characters. People therefore usually react the most strongly to quartertonal intervals, sometimes with great excitement—and sometimes with discomfort, depending on the style in which they're used, and the instrument. (Quarter-tone pianos, for example, can have a jarring effect favored by some, disliked by others.)

Sixthtonal intervals

    Audio Example 4: ascending intervals of 33 to 1233 cents

    Audio Example 5: descending intervals of 33 to 1233 cents

    Audio Example 6: ascending intervals of 67 to 1167 cents

    Audio Example 7: descending intervals of 67 to 1167 cents

    A few observations on sixthtonal intervals: Most sixthtonal intervals are also quite distinct, though they are more subtle than the quartertonal ones. Some musicians say they prefer them for this reason (while others prefer the quarter-tones). In any case, we are more likely to hear sixthtonal intervals in reference to the semitonal intervals that neighbor them, as noticeable, distinctly altered versions of them, rather than as having their own completely unique characters. (But this may not always be the case.)

Also, with sixth-tones we have two points within the semitonal interval spaces, rather than the one point created with quarter-tones. Depending on how they are used, they can combine to illuminate and activate this "middle" pitch region as the quartertone does, but with more nuanced melodic options. (More on this in Part 2.)

Twelfthtonal intervals

    Audio Example 8: ascending intervals of 17 to 1217 cents

    Audio Example 9: descending intervals of 17 to 1217 cents

    Audio Example 10: ascending intervals of 83 to 1183 cents

    Audio Example 11: descending intervals of 83 to 1183 cents

    A few observations on twelfthtonal intervals: As was mentioned earlier, the twelfth-tone itself, 17 cents, can be quite audible and effective as a melodic motion. *Larger* twelfthtonal intervals, on the other hand, are the most subtle type in 72 ET—the minor second plus or minus a twelfth-tone (117 or 83 cents), the major second plus or minus a twelfth-tone (217 or 183 cents), and up. Depending on usage they either can be effectively inaudible (and of questionable musical value) or, alternatively, can add subtle color or feeling. (More on this in Part 2.) When these larger twelfthtonal intervals are noticed at all, they are invariably interpreted as slightly altered, inflected versions of the abutting semitonal intervals. The listening examples and drills here allow easier perception because the intervals are isolated.

Harmonic Understanding

At the risk of influencing students' own newly-forming conceptions of microtonal harmony, I will share some thoughts on how we might hear and classify intervals, in musical terms. Note that the term "harmony" is used in its more ancient sense ("armonia"), where it is a matter of the interval, not the triad, and it includes not just the simultaneous but also the melodic occurrence of intervals. The impressions and insights below are based on various sources: my own composing and teaching, the input of my students, and observations by other composers and performers. Though the ideas might appear subjective, they may nonetheless be of value as they involve shared experiences of musicians spanning a few generations and coming from a range of backgrounds in terms of culture, musical aesthetics, and training. The ideas here are not intended as hard facts or rules, but as the point of view of musicians and as food for thought.

As the new regions in-between the traditional twelve intervals are brought to life by the addition of (especially) quarter-tones and sixth-tones, this prompts us to rethink, more deeply, the old interval identities in this new context, in relation to their new neighbors. As was mentioned in the introduction, when we listen to microtonal music we are unlikely to process the notes we hear according to microtone-type, the way we have been grouping them here for ear training purposes. We hear and understand according to what we already know—12 ET, for most of us. Therefore it makes sense to examine how the new pitches affect our hearing from this familiar vantage point, as we feel the traditional classifications shifting from their ossified positions and forming new alliances.

In his book *Genesis of a Music* Harry Partch listed his own interval categories at the end of Chapter 9 ("The One-Footed Bride"), almost as a side note to the expansive theories that are the main content of his treatise.[11] The categories were as follows: "intervals of approach" (seconds and sevenths), "intervals of emotion" (thirds and sixths), "intervals of suspense" (tritones), and "intervals of power" (fourths, fifths, and octaves). I find these categories aptly descriptive and useful, and I refer to them in this section as a springboard for new ideas (not to appropriate or misuse, I hope). What I appreciate about Partch's classifications is that they are not as reliant on math- or physics-based reasoning as most of the other theory in his book is, but are based more on sensitive listening and observation. I also value the fact that they were formed by someone who was devoted to stripping away the rules of traditional music theory, to developing his own, more authentic understanding. Partch described his interval groupings as "arbitrary categories...according to psychological (or whimsical) reactions."[12] He, too, was using a dense microtonal scale (at that time, of forty-three intervals), and referred in the plural to "tritone intervals," meaning all shades of tritone, "varying amounts of 'second'," and so on. All of this is exactly in the spirit of what I am trying to do, and what I encourage students to do.

The interval groupings below are derived through a listening and thinking process that is somewhat different from the one that shaped the familiar interval groupings of Western diatonic music. Typically those categories have been defined by the following things: *scale degree placement as reflected in the numeric names "second," "third," etc.* (even in atonal music, where the numeric nomenclature remains despite being obsolete)[13], *perception of contrast* (large/major vs. small/minor, also the simplistic mood characterizations happy/major vs. sad/minor in the case of thirds and sixths), and of course *consonant or dissonant classification*. Here there is no assumption of scalar context, so there is no reason to assume, for example, that the intervals formed by C to E-flat and C to E-natural have analogous roles—both "thirds," but of contrasting characters. Without this context, one is left grouping intervals based on the *perception of similarity or connectedness*, rather than contrast. And without consonance and dissonance as the primary consideration, intervals are classified according to more varied descriptive interpretations, as has been discussed—although I restrict my own terms here to general ones such as "emotive" or "powerful" (similar to Partch's terms), leaving finer descriptive characterizations up to the individual.

Nonetheless for ease of communication I still will be using the familiar interval names "minor second," "major third," etc., because they are what most musicians know. Of course, these terms strain to accommodate our new microintervals, and so cents numbers will also be used. (Refer to Figure 1 if necessary.) The cents system has its drawbacks, too—it can seem to require an inconvenient amount of math, and the numbers are dry and lack any descriptive qualities—yet over time it becomes much more efficient in discussions to use numbers. Calling an interval "150" ("one- fifty") is quicker and easier than calling it "a semitone plus a quarter-tone."

Finally, the exact dividing lines between regions aren't necessarily fixed, and could shift by a twelfth-tone here and there. (For example, the "steps of different characters" region could be heard as including 150 cents at its outer limit, not 133 cents.)

Interval Groupings

1. Steps of different characters, clusters (twelfth-tone/minor second region, 17-133 cents): This is the one category in which vertical and horizontal functions are separate and different, just as they always were in tonal contexts, where vertical seconds were strictly-handled dissonances but melodic seconds were favored for fluid, step-wise motion. Partch's term "intervals of approach" for the seconds is certainly a reference to their special "step"-like melodic qualities. The difference here is our narrower range of 17 to 133 cents (large minor second); Partch included major seconds, whereas I attribute "skipping" qualities to those intervals, too, and therefore put them in the next grouping. As melodic elements the new microintervals in this "step" range can have strikingly different characters, as can be heard in a quick comparison of melodic intervals such as 17 cents, 50 cents, 67 cents, 133 cents.

Heard concurrently, the intervals in this range create beats at rates that make it difficult to distinguish separate pitches. Therefore as simultaneities these intervals are better described as "clusters" than as "harmonies." Here it can be *hard* to identify the differences in character mentioned above, between, say, 50 cents and 67 cents—though if they are sustained long enough perhaps we may observe a change in the frequency of the beats.

2. Emotive step-skips (major second/minor third region, 150-350 cents): The intervals that fall within this category often are bound together in our perception. They are a group of intervals that are favored by composers for their rich, emotive qualities, and that often are featured at expressive cadential moments in the scales of Middle Eastern music. Partch's designation "intervals of emotion" seems excellent for this group, even though Partch included the major thirds (not included here), as well as their inversions as sixths, and he did not include the major second intervals. Partch's grouping corresponds with the classification traditionally designated "imperfect consonances," though he was describing character rather than degree of consonance. My grouping, also defined only by character, simply makes the range smaller (just as it does with the "step").

In melody these intervals overlap the functions of "step" and "skip," able to

18

be either. We already know that the minor third, as augmented second, has traditionally been used in certain diatonic contexts as a step—a motion from one scale degree to the next (for example in the "harmonic minor" scale or the Hijaz Maqam). What might seem new is the notion of major second as skip when heard melodically, or as "harmonious" when heard vertically, since traditionally major seconds have been grouped with minor seconds simply as "dissonances," whose harmonic function and meaning is essentially interference. Yet the "size" of the major second increases in our perception when it is surrounded by many smaller intervals; we are aware of more pitches occurring within its space, and thus in melody we can experience it as a *skipping* motion. Furthermore, the major second intervals, when heard as simultaneities, can be perceived as harmonies, not as mere clusters, because we can discern both pitches as separate and relating to each other, and the beating of partials is much less intense than with smaller intervals. Many microtonal musicians, including both Ezra Sims and Joseph Maneri (independently) have even stated that the major second intervals feel "consonant."[14]

Notice the severing of the alliance that the minor third traditionally has had with major third in music theory, and its unexpected grouping with the major second. Yet for the ear on its own maybe those old categories have never been self-evident. College freshman solfege students, even those with stronger skills, even in simple diatonic music, routinely confuse the major second and minor third, but almost never confuse the minor third and major third. (Errors this common and this specific can be instructive about how we hear.)

Our new intervals of 233 cents, 250 cents, and 267 cents form the heart of this expressive region. These intervals completely blur the old line between step/dissonance and skip/consonance, and are richly emotive in a new way. (See Laurent Martin *Trio*, Audio Example 14, which features a theme with many 250-cent skips.)

3. Powerful leaps (major third/perfect fourth region, 367-533 cents, and perfect fifth region, 667-733 cents): The term "perfect intervals" traditionally has been used for fourths and fifths (as well as unisons and octaves) to separate them as a special type of consonance. To include the major third in the same category is new, yet I was interested to hear composer Laurent Martin make this claim about it when he was giving a presentation on his music at the New England Conservatory in 2012; it seemed to be a compelling new perspective on this interval that has for so

19

many centuries been the focus of speculation. How can we describe the collective effect of these intervals in musical terms? It is not meant here so much as a measure of degree of consonance in the old functional sense (even if it can be determined as such); rather the importance is in its dramatic effect, which is bold and lacks the richness and depth of character of the major seconds, minor thirds, sixths and minor sevenths, and perhaps is better characterized by Partch's term "intervals of power" (even though Partch did not include major thirds in this category).

The 350-cent "neutral third" and the neighboring 333 and 367 cents are enjoyed by many musicians, perhaps again because they straddle functions—the expressive role of the smaller "minor third" and the power of the larger "major third." The intervals in this area are familiar to many also as the "blue notes" that are characteristic on the thirds in blues scales. These often are interpreted as the third degree of the major pentatonic scale bent downward to give it more *feeling*, or an often-cited "mournful" quality. Perhaps it also could be described as a way of ridding the major third of some of its inherent brashness or two-dimensionality.

4. Unstable, powerful leaps, bound to fourths and fifths (tritone region, 550-650 cents): Partch's term "intervals of suspense" for the tritones is hard to argue with; the tritone seems to be almost universally felt as unresolved and suspenseful. Because of their instability, one could hear the intervals in the tritone region as dependent on and thus bound to the neighboring fourths and fifths. Maybe they could also be thought of as "unstable intervals of power." So assertive is the instability of this interval, in fact, that it "swallows up" micro-differences of twelfth- or sixth-tone; it can be exceptionally difficult to tell apart the intervals in the range of 567-633 cents, whether they're heard in melody or as simultaneities. At around 550 and 650 cents, on the other hand, they begin to have their own identities, and they bridge the functions of "unstable sound" and "powerful sound" in a way that's curious and compelling to the ear.

5. Emotive leaps, bound to fifths (minor sixth region, 750-833 cents): These intervals, too, seem to have a special attachment to the fifths, more than they do to their other neighbors, the major sixths. They move effortlessly inward to form the fifth, whereas a bit of force is required to move them outward to form major sixths. Minor sixths have always been popular as expressive gestures in tonal music, and they are included by Partch in his category of "intervals of emotion."

6. Emotive leaps (major sixth/minor seventh region, 850-1050 cents):
The intervals in this range also are bound together, and in 12 ET major
sixths and minor sevenths also are routinely confused by young college
solfege students—far more so than minor sixths are with major sixths, or
minor sevenths with major sevenths. They are rich and expressive sonorities
with a more open sound as larger melodic leaps or vertical harmonies.
(Those concerned with pure harmonies may be interested to note that the
interval formed by the seventh harmonic and fundamental, the 969-cent
minor seventh, is near the center of this expressive region, and of course is
just two cents from our 72 ET interval of 967 cents.)

7. Variations on the octave (octave/near-octave region 1067-1333 cents):

Paradoxically, the major seventh and minor ninth, two intervals that
traditionally are considered highly dissonant, can be heard as very similar to
the octave, which is considered the most consonant interval after the unison.
(Ask a young solfege student to sing you a major seventh or a minor ninth,
and she's quite likely to sing an octave, completely unaware of the error.) A
beautiful musical illustration of the octave/ninth association is in Ivan
Wysch- negradsky's quarter-tone piano piece *Etude sur les mouvements
rotatoires* (1961). Wyschnegradsky's "non-octave" concept included the use
of what he called "dilated octaves," i.e. the minor ninth as a kind of stand-in
for the octave. He used this idea very effectively in the opening of that piece,
which begins with stacks of his 650-cent "minor fifths" combining to form
minor ninths. The effect is one that *simulates* the octave with delicately off-
kilter, expanded octaves (not dissonances), spinning outward to infinity—a
concept that was important for Wyschnegradsky.

Figure 4. Interval groupings illustrated on the staff with Middle C as reference.

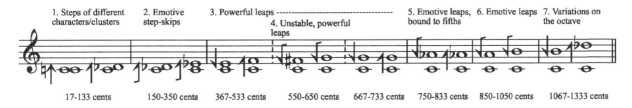

Seeing the intervals grouped this way, according to observed similarities and
connections, it might make sense that the fault lines separating groups are located
where they are—between the minor and major seconds, thirds, sixths and
sevenths—since these are all the same spots where, in the tonal music that is
ubiquitous in the world around us, we are used to distinguishing conspicuous
differences in character. These are also the spots in tonal music where chromatic

pitches often are used to create dramatic intensity—and they are a challenge to sing. It could even be said that I am simply describing the same old listening and performing experiences according to different criteria. My groupings, as it happens, also line up neatly with the areas within the seven diatonic modes where semitones occur (the twelfth-tone/minor second region corresponding with the lower semitone in the Phrygian mode, the major second/minor third region with the lower semitone in Aeolian and Dorian, and so on), and the dividing points fall where they *never* occur (again, between major and minor seconds, thirds, sixths and sevenths). Though the arrangement of semi- and whole tones in the diatonic modes has theoretical origins in the circle of fifths, from the musician's angle semitone-steps in scales are experienced as loci of increased momentum, "leading-tone" or "tendency-tone" motion, spots where pitch connec- tions occur more readily. Whether it is because of musical-cultural influences or due to something more innate, these *non-diatonic, microtonal* groupings appear to reflect similar nexuses of increased attraction within the octave space, regions where the pitches seem to have a sort of magnetic pull toward each other.

Part 2: Composing and Hearing

Preliminary Advice

The exercises in Part 2, like those in Part 1, are grouped by microinterval type: first only quartertonal intervals, then only sixthtonal intervals, then twelfthtonal intervals, mostly in combination with sixth- and quartertonal intervals—full 72 ET. Before beginning, please note the following points of general advice:

• **Composition exercises as ear training:** While the exercises here are intended as exploratory first steps in microtonal composition, they also should be considered a continuation of the ear training. Always sing what you write, or play it on your instrument, or both. The ideal setting is to work with a partner or in a small group of musicians, in order to hear multiple lines and harmonies, and to share impressions. (If this is not possible, using software that enables microtonal playback of multiple lines is a second-best alternative.)

Furthermore, you should make good use of the recordings provided of the examples, performed accurately and with sensitivity by violist Mat Maneri (son of Joseph Maneri), who is one of the great experts in microtonal performance. In addition to enabling you to hear the examples, these recordings also provide you with further exercises for practice, to play back in imitation and refine your ear training skills.

• **Analysis of your own writing:** As a concluding step to every exercise, your own analysis of what you've written will be invaluable, and is modeled in many of the exercise instructions. This includes technical matters, such as labeling every interval, and interpretive ones, your impressions of how the exercises sound and how the pitches interact, using whatever types of terms are most useful for you (with either theoretical or emotive language).

• **An open mind for pitch organization:** You are encouraged to approach the composing exercises with no preformed ideas about pitch organization. It is better to avoid the facile use of structures that belong to the world of 12 ET music and are derived from either tonal or atonal styles with their own systems of functionality or logic. We can compare the new intervals to characters introduced in a play; listen to them carefully and allow them to develop their own type of behavior.

• **An open mind for rhythm:** Likewise, regarding rhythm, in the melodic and contrapuntal writing exercises you may use meter or not—as you wish—but in either case always let your rhythmic choices be inspired by the pitches and intervals rather than applying preexisting rhythmic formulas from older styles, which often fall into rote patterns. French microtonal composer Alain Bancquart has eloquently explained the need for a different, more sensitive approach to rhythm: "As a consequence of the perfect coherence of the tonal world, not only a tonal harmony, but a tonal way of conceiving of rhythm exist. This rhythmic conception is based on cadential thought, repetition, and symmetry: sequences of four or eight equal measures demonstrate an organization of either binary or ternary values. ...My aim is to indicate that a universe that uses as a reference intervals other than the semitone cannot be, from the temporal point of view, based on the relationship solely between two and three."[15] Ivan Wyschnegradsky, writing on the same matter in his *La loi de la pansonorité*, addressed the need to find rhythms that are "more nuanced and more complex" and "at the same time more natural," to match the tiny nuances of pitch in microtonal ("ultrachromatic") systems. He pointed out that since "space and time are inseparable," when we transform musical space with finer octave divisions, we also need to transform time—and he called this a "liberating rhythmic revolution."[16] My own teacher and mentor Joseph Maneri described the same need in terms of the unpredictable motions of a snake, and called this approach to rhythm "snake time." For my part, I feel it to be an approach in which the natural—and often irregular—contours of human physical motion and speech are reflected in much finer detail in both pitch and rhythm, simultaneously.

Quarter-tone Writing Exercises

As was noted earlier, the twenty-four-note quarter-tone scale offers us the most striking new sonorities, and therefore it can be very satisfying to work with. Yet since half of its content are the twelve familiar semitonal intervals and the other half are the quartertonal ones, it also can be a rigid scale to work with. As soon as we try to put all the pitches together and make music we encounter what seems to be a built-in polarity; our sounds seem to be always either "in/old" (semitonal) or "out/new" (quartertonal).[17] Unless our aim is to make our music display this "either/or" sensibility (as a lot of early quartertonal music did, for example much of the work of Julián Carrillo and Alois Hába), it's best to try to move beyond this dichotomy, to feature the new quartertonal sounds in some kind of integrated way with the old semitonal sounds. The exercises below are designed to illuminate this issue.

Exercise 1-A. Motifs using quarter-tones in an ornamental way
Instructions: Compose a few different melodic figures—motifs—in which quarter-tones have an ornamental function. Identify all intervals in cents, with a mark indicating upward or downward motion, as shown in the examples. This step will be important in all writing exercises, to ensure that you are always conscious of your intervals. (Some find it helpful at first to take an additional step and jot down on the side a quick, shorthand "translation" from cents language to the more familiar, traditional language of intervals. For example, 450 cents as "M3/P4," or, later, 417 or 433 cents as "Large M3." This is demonstrated in Figures 5-8.)

What is it about the treatment of quarter-tones in Figure 5 that makes them ornamental, i.e. of secondary function to the semitonal intervals? Their rhythmic placement on the upbeat and their shorter duration are both factors that make them sound fleeting and de-emphasized. The basic contour of this motif is felt to be the semitonal intervals created by the E, F, C and A-flat (minor second, perfect fourth, and minor sixth), because of the rhythmic placement of those pitches on all of the strong beats, enhanced by a bit of syncopation in the first measure, and also by their being both the highest and lowest pitches, and of longer duration.

Figure 5. Motif with ornamental use of quarter-tones.

Audio Example 12

Exercise 1-B. Motifs using quarter-tones in a structural way
Instructions: Compose a few more motifs in which quarter-tones have a structural function. What makes the quartertonal intervals in Figure 6 more structural, more central to the identity of the motif? In this motif they are the ones receiving emphasis through various means, such as rhythmic placement (including syncopation), repetition, longer durations (including the first pick-up note), and register (highest and lowest pitches). In these ways the intervals of 50 cents, 250 cents, and 150 cents are the ones that define the sound of the motif, while semitonal intervals still have an important presence, forming an audible minor third—300 cents—between the lowest and highest pitches (raised D-sharp and lowered G) and a minor second between the E and the F.

Figure 6. Motif with structural use of quarter-tones.

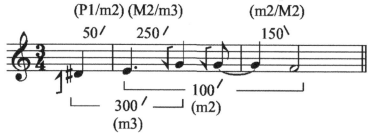

Audio Example 13

In his under-recognized book *Manuel d'harmonie a quarts de ton* (1932), Ivan Wyschnegradsky addressed a similar concern.[18] He devoted the first section of his book to describing and illustrating quarter-tones used as "accidentals" (ornamental neighboring tones, chromatic passing tones), and the second section to quarter-tones used "as an organic part of a musical system."

The lesson of these first motivic exercises is simple and elemental, and could be considered one of the most important offered here—that the stimulating sounds of our new intervals can be intrinsic to the *character and structure* of our music, and that this simply requires attention to various ways of emphasizing the relationships between pitches—rhythm, register, dynamics, articulation. This of course can be the basis of an entire approach to melodic writing or improvising with microtones, and applies equally to writing with sixth- and twelfth-tones, or with any other type of microinterval.

Audio Example 14: Laurent Martin *Trio* (quarter-tones intrinsic to melody)
Audio Example 15: Joe Maneri, Mat Maneri, Barre Phillips "Bonewith" from *Tales of Rohnlief* (various microintervals intrinsic to melody)

Exercise 2-A. Two-part homophonic quartertonal phrases
Prefatory comments: In the exercises below, as we practice carefully putting notes together with two voices, comparisons to traditional counterpoint and part-writing exercises are inevitable, and we might wonder to what extent the centuries-old voice-leading concerns matter here. The only principles that always can be asserted are those unchanging ones that have to do, not with pitch and interval quality, but with our sense of line, motion, register and texture, namely the following:

- That contrary motion generally keeps two lines sounding independent from each other.
- That parallel motion tends to make lines sound less independent, more bound together, especially when it occurs several times in succession.

- That the closer together two or more lines are, in register, the more vivid their interaction is, resulting in richer and more potent sonorities.
- That when two lines overlap, the ear can become confused about which voice is which.
- That in a texture of more than two lines, we hear the highest and lowest lines most clearly. (Though here there will be just two lines.)

What *cannot* be asserted, and must be left up to the individual, as we saw in Part 1, are questions of pitch and interval—how we interpret the sonorities. The hope is that you may be guided by your own new interval charts, and possibly by some of the observations in the discussion under "Harmonic Understanding." Insofar as consonance/dissonance are priorities, or can even be classified, one must make one's own aesthetic choices about how to treat them in the voice-leading, in terms of tension and resolution, parallel motion, leaps, etc.

Instructions: Compose a few homophonic, two-voice progressions of four or five vertical dyads, using a mixture of quartertonal and semitonal pitches, exploring any quartertonal intervals you are interested in. Use a good balance of types of motion (contrary, similar, parallel). The range between the two voices should not exceed two octaves. (If they are within one octave the sonorities will be more intense.) Identify all intervals, harmonic and melodic, in cents, as shown.

Notice that the two voices could interact in a variety of ways. The two lines could alternate quartertonal and semitonal pitches in parallel, resulting in all quartertonal lines and all semitonal harmonies, as in Figure 7. (Note that it's not that the vertical intervals are the same and moving in parallel motion, but simply that the pitches in both voices at the same time are either from the semitonal or the quartertonal domain.) The quartertonal and semitonal pitches could be isolated between the two voices continuously, resulting in all-semitonal lines and all-quartertonal harmonies, as in Figure 8.

Figure 7. Homophonic phrase with all-quartertonal lines and all-semitonal harmonies.

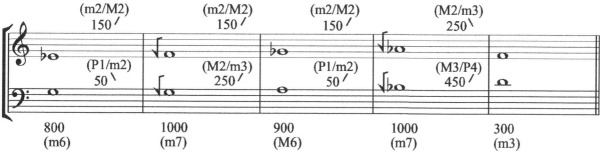

Audio Example 16

Figure 8. Homophonic phrase with all-semitonal lines and all-quartertonal harmonies.

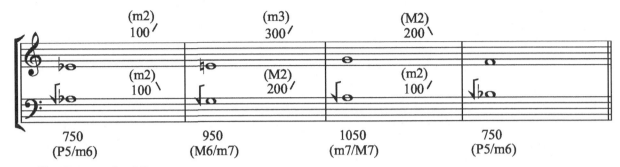

Audio Example 17

The two approaches described above and illustrated in the examples are quite limiting in that they confine intervals to either the horizontal or the vertical plane based on whether they are quartertonal or semitonal, again reinforcing a polarity that is un- necessarily restrictive in a musically arbitrary way. Yet they are worth noting, and perhaps trying, because they demonstrate something important in a new light: the influence of voice-leading, which is linear and horizontal, on our perception of vertical harmony, and the reverse of this. In Figure 7, notice that our perception of the vertical intervals at the moments of arrival on each new dyad—always a standard semitonal interval—is colored by the melodic intervals, which are always quartertonal. The final minor third has a distinct and unfamiliar effect, having been approached by 250 cents in the upper voice and 450 cents in the lower voice. How to describe this effect is a subjective matter (smaller? richer? distorted? some color?), but what's certain is that the linear intervals assert their own quartertonal identities over the vertical ones. With Figure 8 notice, in turn, how the quartertonal vertical sonorities alter our perception of each semitonal interval in either line. Though this can be heard throughout, a particularly noticeable example is the motion from the second dyad to the third; here we cannot hear the upper line motion as a minor third in the familiar sense, or the lower line as a familiar major second. Those melodic progressions feel like *something else* at the moment of arrival on the third dyad. The altered sensation is enhanced in this case by the upward (similar) motion in both voices, and also by the fact that the upper voice has a G natural, and in the preceding dyad the lower voice had a G one quarter-tone lower.

Of course, a less restrictive approach, one more conducive to composer choice, is for the quartertonal and semitonal pitches to be varied in both voices—a free mixture of quartertonal and semitonal harmonies, as in Figure 9. Even more choice, more musicality, more nuance in pitch relationships are possible with the contrapuntal arrangements of these progressions in Exercise 2-B, which adds the element of rhythm.

Figure 9. Homophonic phrases with free mixture of semi- and quartertonal lines and harmonies.

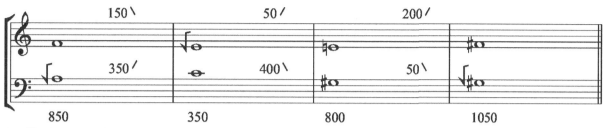

Audio Example 18

Exercise 2-B. Contrapuntal arrangements of the two-part homophonic quartertonal phrases

Instructions: Use your favorite progressions from Exercise 2-A to write contrapuntal phrases. Keep the note values and rhythms large and simple (mostly whole, half, and dotted half notes and rests), and keep the tempo moderately slow. Label all harmonies in cents, including the new harmonies created by the rhythmic movement. Listen and observe as pitches overlap, relationships shift, and we have feelings of suspension and change.

In Figure 10, though there is some alternating of quartertonal and semitonal intervals at the beginning, the semitonal intervals are not necessarily experienced or intended as stable resolutions of the quartertonal ones. A musician might approach quartertonal intervals (and other types of microintervals) with the assumption that they're all "dissonant," but do we really hear them all this way? In measures 1 and 2, is the 850-cent interval dissonant, and the perfect fourth that follows a consonant resolution— even though fourths often are not felt as consonances—simply by virtue of its being a *familiar* interval? Could the "neutral third" at the end of measure 2 feel more consonant than the perfect fourth that precedes it? Here we find illustrated the issues discussed in Part 1: by the mere addition of quartertones, the relationships already are becoming too complex to describe according to the old concepts and terms. The previously unused realms in-between interval classes open up and expand in our perception, and the old, definitive borders between categories become blurred. We see that as we listen, our experience and understanding of these sounds is influenced by their context within the surrounding intervals, not only by the more obvious factors as general familiarity and unfamiliarity, or beating of partials.

Figure 10. Contrapuntal arrangement of Figure 9.

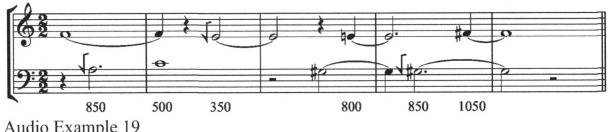

850   500   350   800   850   1050

Audio Example 19

Exercise 3-A. Quartertonal scales

Prefatory comments: Here we experiment with the creation of entire scales with characteristic features, searching for identities that can have musical value for us when used for melody or harmony. The mathematical combinations may immediately appear enticing as we find new symmetries, modes of limited transposition, quartertonal "versions" of older scale contours (octatonic, whole tone, even diatonic, such as Wyschnegradsky's "diatonicised chromatic" scale[19]), "non-octave" scales, and so on. For instance, it can be fun alternating quarter-tones with semitones or whole tones, as in Figures 11 and 12.

Figure 11. Scale with alternating quarter-tone and semitone steps.

50 100 50 100 50 100 etc.

Figure 12. Scale with alternating quarter-tone and whole tone steps.

50   200   50   200   50 etc.

Or we can alternate 150 cents with semitones or whole tones, as in Figure 13.

Figure 13. Scale with alternating three-quarter-tone and semitone steps.

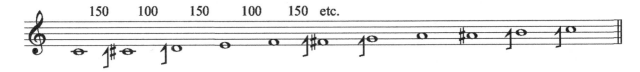

150   100   150   100   150 etc.

Or we can make a scale of all 150-cent steps, as in Figure 14.

Figure 14. Scale with all three-quarter-tone steps.

However, as fascinating as these are to see and contemplate, they are formulas derived from abstract structural concepts, and do not originate with the ear. Of much greater musical value will be scales born of the ear and mind, carefully chosen note for note because of an attraction to certain *characteristic intervals*.[20] This is achieved through the messy process of tinkering, rearranging, always singing or playing, and contemplating the sound of your intervals.

Instructions: Create a few quartertonal scales that span the full octave and consist of two hexachords, each of which roughly spans a fourth. There should be a mixture of quarter- and semitonal pitches, and the steps in your scale should never be larger than 250 cents. Your hexachords should bring out characteristic intervals that you are interested in, especially quartertonal ones. In any scale we'll look not just at steps—the intervals formed by adjacent pitches—but also at relationships among the other scales degrees that are of interest to the ear. In the asymmetrical scale in Figure 15, in addition to the 50-, 100-, 150- and 250-cent steps, the interior intervals of 200, 250, 350, and 450 are the relationships of interest as we move to Part B of the exercise.

Figure 15. Scale with free mixture of quartertonal and semitonal steps.

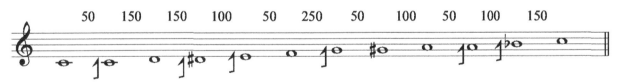

Audio Example 20

Exercise 3-B. "Teaching melodies" with the quartertonal scales
Instructions: With each of your scales (or with only your favorite ones), write a short melody in two phrases, aiming to make it a way to teach your scale—a "teaching melody." One phrase should be comprised of pitches from the bottom hexachord and the other of pitches from the top hexachord (though not necessarily occurring in that order), and the melody should reinforce the identity of each hexachord as a set of pitches with its characteristic intervals—especially those of interest to you. It should be simple enough to learn without too much difficulty.

Repetition of certain pitches or pairs of pitches is a good idea in this assignment, as well as keeping to simple, fluid rhythms. Limit note and rest values to mostly whole-, half-, dotted half-, and quarter-notes, and make your rhythmic choices sensitive to the intervals and how you wish to bring them out.[21]

Label all adjacent intervals in cents, but also examine the relationships formed by certain non-adjacent pitches. In Figure 16, in addition to the striking consecutive intervals such as 350, 100 and 250 cents in the opening and 250 cents at the end, there are other strong relationships such as the interval of 450 cents between the downbeats of the first two measures, the third iteration of the 250-cent relationship between the raised E and the D on the downbeats of measure three and four, and the quarter-tone formed between the raised C at the end of the first phrase and the C that was at the very beginning. Awareness of these larger-scale pitch relationships, as well as the contiguous ones, is basic to all melodic writing, and the new microintervals must be regarded in this light as well.

Figure 16. "Teaching melody" for scale from Figure 15.

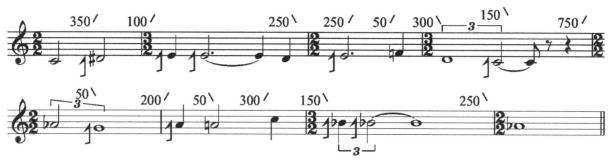

Audio Example 21

Sixth-tone Writing Exercises

In order for the music truly to be in 36 ET, the score must show a mixture of upward- and downward-pointing arrows (to put it in simplistic terms), in combination with pitches from 12 ET. If we were to use only one type, e.g. only sixth-tone-raised pitches in combination with 12 ET pitches, the result would simply be another type of 24 ET, and this would be difficult to distinguish in our writing from quartertonal writing. As was discussed in Part 1, with sixthtonal writing there is no longer the same dichotomy as there is with quartertonal writing, since the sixthtonal pitches and intervals now outnumber the semitonal ones, two to one. The question becomes how adjacent 33-cent and 67-cent intervals relate to *each other,* in our ear, as much as it is how either 33-cent or 67-cent intervals relate to the adjacent semitonal intervals.

Exercise 4. Rewriting quartertonal motifs using sixth-tones
Instructions: The exercise below is a simple and effective introduction to show
how the landscape changes when we shift away from quarter-tones to sixth-tones.
Choose one of your quartertonal motifs from Exercise 1-B and use its contour as
the basis for a new motif in 36 ET, using a combination of semitonal pitches and
sixthtonal pitches of *both* types—raised and lowered. Identify all intervals in cents.
Notice that in Figure 17 the quartertonal symbols from Figure 6 have not simply
been replaced with sixthtonal ones; once the sixth-tones are introduced, they
suggest a new direction for the motif, and the F is raised. This creates the distinct
ending interval of 133 cents from the lowered G, perhaps closer to the effect of the
150-cent ending of the original version, whereas to return to an F natural might
evoke more of a familiar, "normal" minor third to major second sound. Yet,
listening to both Figure 6 and Figure 17, we can hear that they have noticeably
different characters, even though the contour has been preserved and the
adjustments appear so small.

Figure 17. Sixthtonal arrangement of quartertonal motif from Figure 6.

Audio Example 22

Exercise 5-A. Hexachords mixing semitonal and sixthtonal pitches
Prefatory comments: As was the case with the quartertonal scales, our aim here is
to develop our sense of scalar or pitch set identity, and characteristic intervals.
However, with the greater number of pitches and denser texture in 36 ET, our
approach in this section will be slightly changed. Smaller pitch collections,
hexachords, will be our emphasis, rather than scales spanning the full octave, so
that we can focus on the more intricate pitch relationships, and the exercises will
follow a somewhat different process. As you rearrange your hexachords again and
again in these exercises, all the while listening, notice as you begin to internalize
the special identity or mood of each one.

Instructions: Create a few hexachords combining semitonal pitches and sixthtonal
pitches of both types—raised and lowered—focusing on interesting combinations.
Keep the total range within roughly a perfect fifth, from lowest pitch to highest,
and keep the scale steps no larger than 233 cents. Label the intervals in cents.

Figure 18. Hexachord mixing semitonal and sixthtonal pitches (raised and lowered).

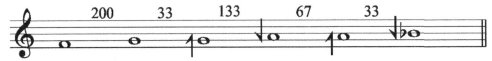

Audio Example 23

Exercise 5-B. Hexachord reorderings
Instructions: For each one of your hexachords write three separate reorderings of the pitches (using whole notes), still seeking interesting intervallic combinations, which now involve non-adjacent scale pitches. You may find during this stage that you wish to change a note or two in your hexachord. Label the intervals in cents.

Figure 19. Reorderings of hexachord from Figure 18.

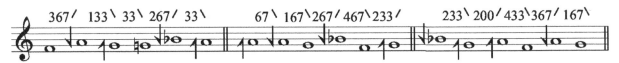

Audio Example 24

Exercise 5-C. Rhythmic arrangements of the hexachord reorderings
Instructions: For each one of your re-orderings, write a rhythmic arrangement of the pitches, creating a short melodic phrase. Again, make your rhythmic choices simple, and make them respond to the intervals and how you want to bring them out. In phrase 1 of Figure 20, downbeat accent, duration, and syncopation are used to bring out the ascending intervals of 367 and 267 cents, as well as the downward motions of 133 cents and 33 cents (twice—in measures two and three). Phrase 2 isolates the ascending intervals of 267 and 233 cents formed by contiguous pitches in measures two and three, using longer durations on the higher notes, as well as rests, but in those measures our ear is also drawn to the interval of 233 cents formed by the non- adjacent lowered B-flat and raised G, as well as the interval of 200 cents between the G natural and the F. Phrase 3 emphasizes a downward progression that sounds microtonally chromatic, from downbeat to downbeat (including syncopation with ties) of 33 cents (lowered B-flat to raised A) and 67 cents (raised A to lowered A), ending with a cadential use of 167 cents from the lowered A to the G natural. We may again be measuring this G against the F in measure two, since they are both lower notes in the contour, though the F is in a rhythmically weaker spot, and the repeating of the lowered A brings more attention to that pitch's relationship to the final G.

Figure 20. Rhythmic arrangements of hexachord reorderings from Figure 19.

Audio Example 25

Exercise 5-D. Two-voice arrangements of the hexachords
Instructions: Write a few two-voice arrangements of these same hexachords, keeping the upper and lower halves of your scale separated between the two voices in order to limit the range and preserve the sense of line in each voice. You can mix around the order of the three pitches freely in either voice by seeking interesting combinations both melodically and harmonically, as in Figure 21. This example uses a mix of contrary and similar motion for a feeling of variety and independence between the voices, as the harmonies move around in the in-between territories of small major seventh, enlarged minor sixth, enlarged fifth, and finally from the large major sixth to the next-larger interval of small minor seventh. This ending is an example of something discussed earlier: the final interval of 967 cents is heard in relation to the interval just before it, 933 cents, not as "measured" against a 12 ET point of reference. The emotive harmonic region between the major sixth and minor seventh is thus brought to life in a way that is stimulating to the ear, as can be felt in the peculiar sort of resolution on that final pitch.

Another approach is to keep similar/parallel motion by using all ascending or all descending order in both voices, as in Figure 22, which can have a kind of cat and mouse effect as the lines chase each other upwards, or to keep contrary motion by using all ascending order in one voice and all descending in the other, as in Figure 23, which creates an ever denser texture as it progresses inward. The two voices can be kept within one octave of each other, for more generally dense sonorities, or separated by an octave for a more open sound, as in Figure 24. Again the rhythms should be subtle; use whole notes, half notes, dotted halves, occasional quarter notes, and occasional rests. Be conscious of which intervals you wish to emphasize or de- emphasize. Label all intervals in cents—horizontal and vertical.

Figure 21. Free contrapuntal arrangement of hexachord from Figure 18 (bottom three notes in upper voice, top three notes in lower voice).

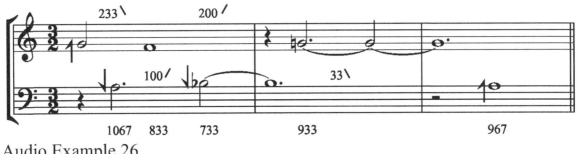

Audio Example 26

Figure 22. Contrapuntal arrangement of hexachord from Figure 18 with similar motion (bottom three notes in lower voice, top three notes in upper voice).

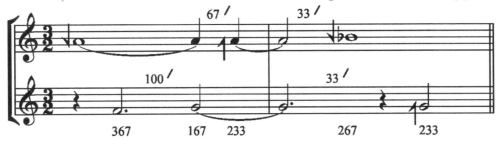

Audio Example 27

Figure 23. Contrapuntal arrangement of hexachord from Figure 18 with contrary motion.

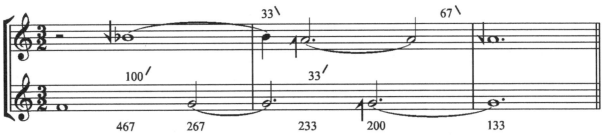

Audio Example 28

Figure 24. Same arrangement from Figure 23 with lower voice an octave below.

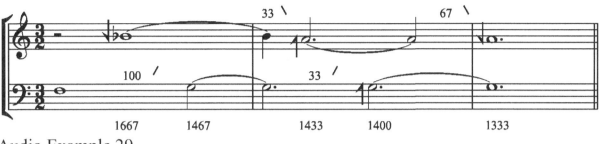

Audio Example 29

Twelfth-tone Writing Exercises

Exercise 6-A. Micromelodic phrases
Instructions: Compose a few short microtonal phrases of four to seven (maximum) notes each. The total range, from highest to lowest pitch, should be *no more than 150 cents*, and there should be at least one melodic twelfth-tone in each phrase (but possibly more), as well as any other microintervals you choose. Continue to be sensitive to the essential role that your rhythms play in supporting and giving meaning to your pitches. In Figure 25, after the relatively large-sounding "skip" of 150 cents, the remainder of the phrase fills in this interval with the gentle descent of a quarter-tone, the expressive upward motion of a twelfth-tone and another downward resolution of a quarter-tone from the raised G to the lowered G. This type of line we could aptly call "micromelody," for it is indeed *melody*; as you listen, notice how much musical distance has been traveled, how much narrative progression has occurred—arguably as much as with any phrase in 12 ET—even though the total range is only 150 cents.

Figure 25. Micromelodic phrase.

Audio Example 30

Exercise 6-B. Expanding the micromelodic phrases
Instructions: Choose some of your phrases from Exercise 6A and expand them with the addition of a second phrase. Maintain the "micromelodic" principle in each phrase by including more melodic twelfth-tones, where appropriate, and melodic sixth- and quarter-tones (as well as seconds and thirds altered by twelfth-, sixth- and quarter-tones) and by keeping the total range limited to no more than

about a perfect fourth. Label all intervals in cents.

Figure 26. Micromelodic phrase from Figure 25, expanded with a second micromelodic phrase.

Audio Example 31

Along with the thrilling new sound of the quarter- and sixthtonal intervals, the possibility of including micromelody in our music is one of the most compelling, radically different, and least explored aspects of working in a fine temperament such as 72 ET. This type of melodic line can expand our musical perception as a microscope reveals to us the world of microorganisms. Even if one doesn't limit entire compositions to linear movements in such a confined range, micromelody can be a powerful new expressive aspect of the music.

Audio Example 32: Joseph Maneri, *Sharafuddin b Yahya Maneri, Makhdum ul Mulk*

Exercise 7. Melody with larger twelfthtonal intervals
Prefatory comments: This exercise explores the melodic use of *larger* twelfthtonal intervals—twelfth-tone alterations of traditional intervals, such as a small or large minor third (283 or 317 cents), small or large perfect fifth (683 or 717 cents), etc. This is the most sensitive aspect of writing in 72 ET, where basic questions of audibility are most critical.

Instructions: Compose three new microtonal phrases of four to seven (maximum) notes each, combining twelfthtonal pitches and semitonal pitches only, to create a mixture of larger twelfthtonal intervals and semitonal ones in a good balance. Do not use sixth-tones or quarter-tones, and do not combine raised twelfth-tone pitches contiguously with lowered twelfth-tone pitches because that produces sixthtonal intervals and the point here is to work with only twelfthtonal intervals, in combination with semitonal.[22] Find ways to bring out the identities of your twelfthtonal intervals as much as possible, always remembering the essential role of rhythm. Mark the interval sizes in cents.

In Figure 27 a few factors enable the microintervals to be heard, albeit as subtle colors: accent due to downbeat placement and syncopation, repetition (of the raised B), and longer duration (including the F# of the 517-cent interval) all play a role in this. Again non-adjacent pitches form important relationships; we hear the raised B in relation to the opening G natural at least as much as we hear it in relation to the A just before it, and thus 417 cents is an important interval here as well as 217 cents. The raised B is also the highest note, which is another factor. The lowered A at the end is quite striking, but this is more due to the strong interval of 233 cents that it forms with this same raised B, two notes earlier, than it is due to the interval of 283 cents it forms with the adjacent F-sharp. Here we see demonstrated the seeming inevitability that twelfth-tone pitches will at some point combine to form audible non-twelfth-tone relationships.

However, even if Figure 27 demonstrates an effective use of larger twelfthtonal intervals, it should nonetheless be noted that the overall effect of these sonorities is quite subtle and fragile; the listener's ability to process them can be compromised by things like instrumental timbre and the natural fluctuations that occur with articulation and breath.

Figure 27. Phrase with larger twelfthtonal intervals, used effectively.

Audio Example 33

Compared with Figure 27, the twelfthtonal intervals in Figure 28 are far less audible, their function much more questionable. Shorter durations, weak metric placement, and the less prominent location of the lowered A in the contour, are again all factors in this, but so is the lower ratio of twelfthtonal to semitonal intervals. If we even notice the twelfthtonal intervals involved in the passing tone figure in measure one (the same 217-cent-sized step as in Figure 27, but shifted down one twelfth-tone) and in the quick leaps much later in measures three and four, we may not know how to interpret them. Was the performer just playing a bit out of tune on two isolated notes? What is the role of these twelfthtonal intervals in the context of this mostly semitonal phrase? (The listener may well have the same problem understanding this phrase if the A and A-flat are altered by sixth-tones or quarter-tones.) Though it may seem counterintuitive, the more the melodic vocabulary is filled with the microintervals, the more the music may "make sense"—as long as the writing is coherent. A composer has much more to work with when twelfth-tones are combined with sixth- and quarter-tones, which enables free movement within the new pitch spaces. This leads us to our last group of exercises, in which we're composing fully in 72 ET. (Twelfthtonal harmonies will be included in the next section.)

Figure 28. Phrase with larger twelfthtonal intervals, used less effectively.

Audio Example 34

"Sporting freely in the whole sea of seventy-two-note possibilities"
Exercise 8-A. Motifs and phrases

Instructions: Compose a distinct motif featuring either a larger quartertonal interval (at least 250 cents), using semitonal and quartertonal pitches, or a larger sixthtonal interval (at least 233 cents) using semitonal and sixthtonal pitches. Then transpose your motif with the featured interval "off the grid" of 24 ET or 36 ET, using the other microtonal symbols, as shown in Figure 29. (The featured 250-cent interval, originally beginning on a repeated A is transposed to begin 467 cents higher, on a sixth-tone lowered D.) Finally, expand your transposed motif into a phrase, as shown. Label all intervals in cents.

Figure 29. Motif featuring a quartertonal skip of 250 cents; transposition of same motif up 467 cents; expansion of transposition into a phrase.

Audio Example 35

Exercise 8-A is designed to help you experiment with freeing your ear and mind from their tether to 12 ET as reference, a tether that is sometimes the result of notational conventions as much as it is of ear training conventions. This is not to imply that it is somehow musically necessary to avoid semitonal pitches or intervals, but rather that we need not rely on them mindlessly, out of habit, as a kind of default position for our music. Intervals of all types, including semitonal ones, should be chosen deliberately, individually and carefully because of their desired sonority. Figure 30 shows a two-phrase variation on the previous examples that integrates all types of intervals, and includes semitonal pitches, as well as

40

semitonal intervals such as the major third formed between the opening A and the C-sharps in measures three and four, and the major second between the lowered D and the lowered E in measures five and six.

Figure 30. Two-phrase melody—first phrase beginning with original motif from Figure 29, second phrase beginning with transposed motif.

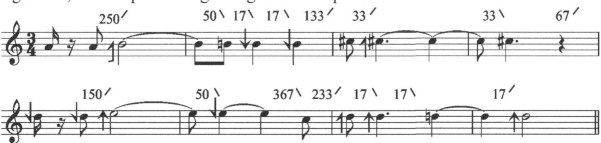

Audio Example 36

Exercise 8-B. Contrapuntal phrases
Instructions: In this assignment we focus on vertical harmonies with free use of all of our 72 ET microinterval types, both horizontally and vertically. Compose a phrase for two voices in which each voice has a line of four to five notes and melodic intervals are never greater than 250 cents. (In Figure 31 both voices are micromelodic.) Use a moderate-to-slow tempo, using mostly longer note values, in a manner similar to Exercises 2-B and 5-D. Use a variety of microtonal harmonies, emphasizing ones that interest you, and *include at least one twelfthtonal vertical harmony in a prominent way*. Label all intervals in cents—horizontal and vertical. Examined in terms of its vertical harmonies, Figure 31 plays with two alternating versions of minor third (the cloudy 333 and the brighter 283) in the middle, framed by a small, expressive major second in the opening and the two larger ("powerful") ending intervals in the major third/perfect fourth region.

Figure 31. Free contrapuntal phrase in 72 ET (maximum step size of 250 cents).

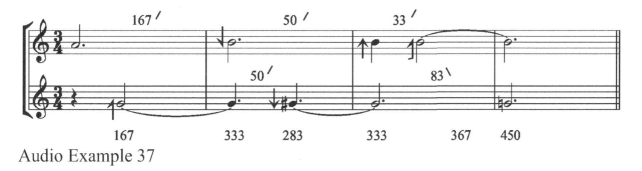

Audio Example 37

41

Exercise 8-C. Hexachords using all types of microintervals
Instructions: Create a few hexachords in 72 ET featuring intervals that interest you and following the guidelines for the 36 ET hexachords in Exercise 5-A—but now combining a variety of types of microintervals, raised and lowered. Each step in the hexachord should be no smaller than 33 cents and no larger than 250 cents. Label all adjacent intervals in cents.

Figure 32. Hexachord in 72 ET.

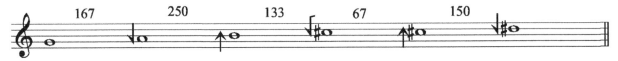

Audio Example 38

With your new hexachords you can follow the steps in Exercises 5-B, 5-C and 5-D, exploring reorderings of your scale pitches, applying rhythm to make phrases, and making two-voice arrangements with the scale divided into top half in one voice and bottom half in the other. Analyze them as modeled for those exercises, observing the new twelfthtonal intervals as well.

Alternatively you can follow the steps in Exercise 3-B, writing a "teaching melody" as shown in Figure 33, aiming to make it a way for a musician to learn your 72 ET hexachord. It should feature the characteristic intervals of interest to you, and be simple enough to learn without too much difficulty.

Figure 33. "Teaching melody" for hexachord from Figure 32.

Audio Example 39

Exercises such as these, based on the hexachords, do not allow for micromelody since the hexachords use larger steps and intervals and the focus is on developing a sense of the identity of the pitch set/scale, which is harder to achieve with intervals grouped within the semitone or whole tone. We can *combine* the two concepts, however. In Figure 34 the teaching melody of Figure 33 is embellished with a single micromelodic flourish.

Figure 34. "Teaching melody" from Figure 33 with added micromelodic flourish.

Audio Example 40

Audio Example 14: *Trio*, by Laurent Martin. Recording used by permission of the composer.
Audio Example 15: "Bonewith," composed and performed by Joe Maneri, Barre Phillips and Mat Maneri. ℗ECM Records 1999. Used by permission of ECM Records GmbH, Munich.
https://www.ecmrecords.com/Catalogue/ECM/1600/1678.php
Audio Example 32: *Sharafuddin b Yahya Maneri, Makhdum ul Mulk*, by Joseph Maneri. Recording used by permission of the Maneri family.
Audio Example 41: *Rain, a Window, Roof, Chimneys, Pigeons and so… and Railway-Bridges, too.* Recording used by permission of the composer.
Audio Example 42: "Concert Piece II" by Ezra Sims, from *Ezra Sims: Musing and Reminiscence*. New World Records #80709-2 ℗2010 © 2010 Anthology of Recorded Music, Inc. Used by permission.
http://www.newworldrecords.org/album.cgi?rm=view&album_id=84351
https://itunes.apple.com/us/album/id393226053
Audio Example 43: "24 Préludes," sixth movement, from *Ivan Wyschnegradsky: Étude sur les mouvements rotatoires, 24 Préludes*. Col Legno Records #20206 ℗2002. Used by permission.
https://www.col-legno.com/de/katalog/gesamtverzeichnis/etude__24_preludes

Endnotes

1   For that matter, microtones enable musical attempts at *animal* expression, or other expressions from the natural or industrial world around us. A nice example is Martin Smolka's *Rain, a Window, Roofs, Chimneys, Pigeons and so... and Railway-Bridges, too* (1993), an enchanting polyrhythmic work using moans, hoots, churnings, and other gestures that evoke an urban landscape. **Audio Example 41**. This piece would have pleased Charles Ives, an early microtonal experimenter who wrote that with quarter-tones we could try "to find out how to use a few more of the myriads of sound waves nature has put around in the air...for man to catch if he can and 'perchance make himself a part with nature'." Ives, Charles, and Howard Boatwright. *Essays before a Sonata: And Other Writings.* New York: W. W. Norton & Company, Inc., 1961. 109.

2   Schoenberg, Arnold. *Theory of Harmony.* Berkeley: University of California, 1978. 424.

3   This is not to say that preconceived theories cannot offer us anything of value. There seems to be no end to the fascinating mathematical possibilities and potential new structures that arise with microtones, and some can lead to compelling musical results. For example, both Ivan Wyschnegradsky and Ezra Sims (independently) have explored the notion that the interval formed by the eleventh partial of the overtone series and the fundamental could function as a substitute or analog for the tonic major triad (formed by the third and fifth partials). The eleventh partial and the fundamental (or eighth partial) together form an interval of a fourth augmented by about a quarter-tone (551 cents). Wyschnegradsky, who called the interval "major fourth" and its inversion (649 cents) "minor fifth," took a philosophical view of it (and of microtonality in general); he viewed quarter-tones as leading to "the conquest and the incorporation into the music of the 11th overtone," just as, in the 15th and 16th centuries, the use of thirds represented the "conquest of the 5th overtone." This idea is thought-provoking and popular, embraced as well by many today in the modern just intonation movement, who speak in terms of "5-limit" music (using the triad), "7-limit" (adding the pure minor seventh) "11-limit" (adding the pure eleventh), and onward. However, from the angle of the music itself, if there is any credibility to the idea that this interval can function in a way comparable to the fifth of a tonic triad it is not because of some innate truth and inevitability, a sort of centuries-long process of humankind evolving upwards through the overtone series. It is because the intervals of 550 cents and 650 cents are so close to the perfect fourth and fifth that we will easily hear them as altered versions of them, and because Wyschnegradsky and Sims are artists who both have known how to make it work this way in their music. Both composers feature this interval prominently as distinct, arresting opening and closing figures and ostinati. (See Sims's *Concert Piece II*, opening and closing of first movement, **Audio Example 42**, and Wyschnegradsky's *24 Préludes en quarts de ton dans l'échelle chromatique diatonisée à 13 sons* (1934/revised 1960/1975), #6, **Audio Example 43**.)

4   Of all the equal temperaments, 48 ET is the one that differs the most since its smallest unit, the eighth-tone (25 cents), is at the exact half-way point in-between our twelfth-tone and our sixth-tone—8.33 cents—and thus demonstrates the largest possible distance from any 72 ET pitch. One could view the issues discussed later regarding twelfth- and sixth-tones (concerning audibility, flexibility of melodic motion, diversity of sound) as combined and embodied together in the eighth-tone, and perhaps even choose 48 ET as a simplified approach to what I am proposing here. Alternatively, if an even finer grid is desired, one could divide the eighth-tone into sixteenth-tones (12.5 cents). However, other than the sixteenth-tone pianos designed by

Juliàn Carrillo and sold by the Sauter Piano company, examples of instrumental performance in sixteenth-tones are hard to find.

5   Aristoxenus' theory was noteworthy during his time also because it differed fundamentally from the approach of the more widespread Pythagorean theory; he proposed a conception of intervals as points on a continuum of pitch rather than as the result of mathematical ratios calculated on strings. It could be said that the linear approach proposed here (which reflects the training of most musicians) differs in the same way from the prevailing approach to microtonality today, in which intervals are derived from frequency ratio calculations.

6   Maneri, Joseph and Van Duyne, Scott. *Preliminary Studies in the Virtual Pitch Continuum*. Plainview, NY: Accentuate Music, 1986; North Adams, MA: Boston Microtonal Society, 2004.

7   Ezra Sims, "Reflections on This and That (Perhaps a Polemic)," *Perspectives of New Music* Volume 29, no. 1 (Winter 1991): 242.

8   Contrary to frequent (and largely unchallenged) claims, it is not realistic to assume that musicians naturally tune their intervals according to pure intervals such as the 5/4 and the 7/4—not even string players. One recent study that appears to support my position on this has been conducted by researcher Till Knipper. Knipper has analyzed numerous rehearsals with violist Garth Knox and other established violists of the first movement ("hora lungă") of György Ligeti's *Sonata for Viola Solo*, a piece that was conceived and written in just intonation. Knipper's study, conducted using phonetic software program Praat, was presented at the Ligeti Symposium in Hamburg in 2012, and it revealed that the 5th, 7th and 11th partials were consistently performed close to 12 ET (in which these musicians, of course, had been trained), not the just tuning.

        http://quintetnet.hfmt-hamburg.de/Ligeti-Symposium/?page_id=156

This study (and similar findings from another study Knipper has made together with Gunter Kreutz of violists performing Klaus Huber's '...*Plainte*...') indicates that even the most skilled players need substantial microtonal ear training and the appropriate musical context in order to perform any microintervals accurately, whether just or not. It does not happen automatically, "naturally," but rather requires intention and practice. As Knipper and Kreutz concluded, "it seems highly likely that a precise mental representation of intervals is a long-term learning process that is highly influenced by the culturally dominant tuning." Till Knipper and Gunter Kreutz, "Exploring microtonal performance of '...*Plainte*...' by Klaus Huber for viola d'amore in third-tone tuning," *Musica Scientiae* (December 2013): 394.

9   http://ada.evergreen.edu/~arunc/texts/music/xenakisFeldman.pdf

10   Composer and scholar James Tenney's excellent book *A History of 'Consonance' and 'Dissonance'* demonstrates that consonance/dissonance classifications throughout history were idiosyncratic and fluid, constantly changing from one period to the next, and from theorist to theorist. These changes were determined by differing musical practices as well as by the varying definitions of consonance (the sense of "fusion" between two tones, the "clarity" of a harmonic interval, the "stability," and eventually, beginning with Helmholtz, the "smoothness"). The complex nature of forming interval categories and the inadequacies of the binary consonance/dissonance concept were reflected in the fact that, especially during the Middle Ages, many theorists needed to create multiple subcategories, including not only perfect and imperfect but also *intermediate* consonances *and* dissonances. The classifications sometimes shifted, too, according to whether an interval was simple or compound. (Tenney, James. *A History of 'Consonance' and 'Dissonance.'* New York: Excelsior Music Publishing Company, 1988.)

11   Partch, Harry. *Genesis of a Music*. New York: Da Capo Press, 1979. 156-57.

12   Ibid., 156.

13   Some serial composers and theorists replaced the diatonic interval names with integer notation for the counting of semitones (0 = unison, 1 = minor second, 2 = major second, etc.). But our *perception* of intervals was not reconsidered with any special insight, other than perhaps using acoustics for new and improved explanations of the same old binary notions of consonance and dissonance. Perhaps microtones are needed to prompt a genuine re-thinking of harmony.

14   The major second was classified as a type of consonance—an "intermediate consonance"—by the late Medieval theorist Jacobus of Liège, who was the author of the largest extant Medieval treatise on music theory, *Speculum Musicae*. Jacobus also classified the minor seventh as an "imperfect consonance." Swiss Theorist Heinrich Glarean in the early sixteenth century also took an accepting view of the major second, writing the following in his teaching manual *Isogoge in musicen*: "The tone [whole tone], in our time, in the nine to eight proportions [the 9/8 ratio] has been banished from the society of the consonances, for just what heinous crime I do not know." (Tenney, James. *A History of 'Consonance' and 'Dissonance'*. New York: Excelsior Music Publishing Company, 1988. 109, 46.)

15   Alain Bancquart. *Une arithmétique de l'anti-système : Deux exemples de combinatoires de chiffres*. Conference of the seminar Mathématiques et musique (MAMUX) at IRCAM, Paris, February15, 2002.

        http://www.musicologie.org/publirem/bancquart.html

16   Ivan Wyschnegradsky. *La loi de la pansonorité*. Genève: Éditions Contrechamps, 1996. 212.

17   Here confusion sometimes arises over microtonal pitches and microintervals, and so an important distinction must be made. Of course, only musicians with absolute pitch can be expected to recognize an individual *pitch* as coming from outside the familiar tuning system. Early microtonal composer Alois Hába, who purportedly had absolute pitch, described *pitches* from the quartertonal domain as "new" and the remaining semitonal domain as "old," and formulated some of his early theories on this premise in his 1927 *Neue Harmonielehre des diatonischen, chromatischen, Viertel-, Drittel-, Sechstel-, und Zwölftel-Tonsystems*. In my experience, musicians with absolute pitch often share this perspective. Such people are the minority, however; for the rest of us, it is primarily the *intervals* that have meaning. Since it is *combinations* of pitches that melodies and harmonies are made up of, we should always keep our attention on the intervals we are creating; we cannot assume that we are "making something microtonal happen" just by placing a microtonal symbol next to a notehead.

18   Ivan Wyschnegradsky. *Manuel d'harmonie à quarts de ton*. Paris, Max Eschig, 1980.

19   Wyschnegradsky built a quartertonal scale with a sequence of semitones and quarter-tones analogous to the contour of the major scale. See composer's preface in Ivan Wyschnegradsky, *24 Préludes en quarts de ton dans l'échelle chromatique diatonisée à 13 sons*. Frankfurt, Belaïeff, 1979.

20   The importance of characteristic intervals to your scale's identity can be compared to the way that the distinct identities of diatonic modes are often described, at least with our modern ears, in terms of their "characteristic steps"—for example the whole step motion from the seventh to eighth scale degrees that many experience as the definitive sound of the Mixolydian mode.

21   The teaching melody might have a similar function, in a sense, to the improvised alap of Hindustani music, which functions to introduce the raga at the beginning of a performance—although the alap comes from an entirely different tradition and has a specific, methodical, note-

by- note manner of revealing the raga.

22   The reader may notice that no exercises have been provided involving *only* twelfthtonal intervals—all "83s" or all "17s"—just as none were provided involving only sixthtonal intervals, and the only all-quartertonal writing was in Figures 7 and 8. From the beginning, up until this point—as we are about to dive in to a full aggregate of all possible interval types—the emphasis has been on introducing the new microinterval types combined with the semitonal intervals. A little bit of experimenting will show that scales built of only "83-cent" intervals, for example, do not result in "83-cent" writing, because as soon as the order of pitches diverges from their arrangement in the scale from lowest to highest, "67s" and "33s" will begin to appear. If *"83-cent" writing* is desired, then the focus would need to be on linear successions of "83-cent" intervals, and on maintaining that sensibility by *avoiding the perception of other microinterval types*, which will be a difficult and probably futile pursuit.

Made in the USA
Middletown, DE
14 September 2022

10432141R00031